A DAY AT THE BEACH

Fiction for Seniors

seniorality

1

chapter 1
A Lovely Idea

THE TABLE is piled high with red ripe strawberries, sweet slices of watermelon, and blueberries that are plump and juicy. I pull out my chair and sit down to enjoy my lunch.

David places a delicate china plate in front of me. The plate holds a tall sandwich full of ham, Swiss cheese, lettuce, and tomato. The tomato was grown in our own backyard and looks smooth and beautiful.

"Thank you," I say to David. "This looks delicious."

I pick up the pickle spear that lies beside my giant sandwich and bite into it. The salty tang of vinegar and seasoning hits my mouth and makes my throat tingle as I swallow.

David joins me at the table, his own plate weighed down with a sandwich that looks like mine. We are sitting together on the sun porch, enjoying the warm summer sunlight while we eat our lunch.

"How does it taste?" David asks.

I have just taken a big bite of my sandwich. Tangy tomato juice runs down my chin and drips onto the yellow tablecloth. Crumbs from the toasted bread also fall to dot the table. I close my eyes and enjoy the taste.

"It is yummy. I am so glad you suggested that we plant tomatoes this year. It really makes this sandwich delicious," I say to David once my mouth is empty.

Outside, a gentle summer breeze makes the leaves on our oak tree shimmer. I watch the pattern of sunlight on the sidewalk shift as the leaves bend and sway. David stands up and opens the door. As soon as he does, the breeze blows past me, ruffling my hair and casusing a napkin to fall to the floor.

"It is such a beautiful day today. I think we should go somewhere," I say to David as I bend to pick up the fallen napkin.

He nods his head and looks out the window for a moment. "How about the beach?" he asks.

My heart leaps. The beach is one of my favorite places to spend time. I am always ready for a trip to the beach. David and I are lucky; we only live about an hour from a lovely little beach.

"Yes!" I say. "Let's pack our bags and go as soon as we finish eating. What a great idea, David."

I finish the food left on my plate and plan in my mind what I should bring on this trip. I'm going to wear my blue bathing suit, for sure. I'll also need to remember to pack a book to read, a towel, and some sunscreen. I begin to get very excited. This will be my first beach trip of the summer. It has been far too long since I've seen the ocean and felt the sand crunch between my toes.

David clears the table and washes our two plates while I head off into the bedroom to pack my things. I reach into the closet and grab my large canvas bag from the shelf. The bag's handles are made of rope and it has a picture of an anchor on the side. It is a perfect bag for a day at the beach.

I put a spray bottle of sunscreen in the side pocket and roll up a bright pink towel. The towel is a gift from an old friend. My birthday was last month, and she knows how much I enjoy the beach, so a huge towel was really a thoughtful gift for me. There is just enough room left in the bag for my paperback book, a pair of sunglasses, and my cell phone.

I slip my bathing suit on and pull an old t-shirt over my head as a cover-up.

"David? Are you ready?" I yell down the hall, as excited as a kid on the first day of summer vacation. He pokes his head around the corner and smiles at me.

"Yep. All ready." He slings his own tote bag over his shoulder and walks down the hall to meet me.

"Let's go, dear," he says and links his arm through mine.

"I think we'll take the convertible today."

chapter 2
Taking a Ride

I AM SO excited at the idea of riding in David's convertible. It is a beautiful car. It is shiny black on the outside with smooth gray leather seats inside. He washes and waxes it every week, to keep the car in good shape.

I watch from the porch as David carefully pulls the car out of the garage. I place my hand above my eyes to block out the blinding sun so that I can see better. David parks in the driveway and I see the trunk pop open.

"Are you packed and ready?" he calls to me as he slides out of the car. I look down at myself. Blue bathing suit - check. Flip-flops - check. I look in my beach bag one last time to make sure I haven't forgotten anything.

"I think I'm all ready," I answer. I walk down the porch steps with my bag over one shoulder. Back in the garage, David starts removing beach chairs from wall hooks. The chairs are the kind that are low to the ground. These are comfortable for me to sit in at the ocean's edge and let the water wash over my feet.

David carries one chair in each hand and puts them in the car's trunk. I lift my bag up and set it on top of the chairs. I feel as happy as a child on vacation.

"Where is your bag, David?" I ask.

"Just inside the house. Let me grab it and lock the door then we can get going."

He opens the passenger door for me and I ease myself down into the comfortable seat. David leans across me and pushes a button on the dash. He grins at me and hurries off to get his things from inside the house. I hear an electric hum and the roof of the car begins to slide back.

Golden sunlight splashes onto my lap and warms my face as the gap in the car's top widens. Once the roof is open all the way the car becomes quiet. I close my eyes and lean back against the seat. I put my sunglasses on and wait for David to return.

Only a moment later, I hear the trunk click shut and then David is sitting beside me, turning the key and starting the engine.

"Beach, here we come," he says.

David honks the horn and waves as we pass our neighbor's house. Our neighbor is outside watering his grass. I lift my hand to wave also as we roll slowly down the quiet street. Once we're out of the neighborhood, David reaches down and turns on the radio. My ears are filled with upbeat music, and I bob my head and shoulders to the beat.

Soon we're on the highway driving fast, the wind blowing my short hair back off my face. We have turned the music up louder to hear it over the rush of the wind and I am still dancing in my seat. In no time, I smell a hint of salt in the air and, as David rounds a curve, the long, winding coastline comes into view.

On this coast, there are very few hotels and only a few houses, so the view is clear. The road we're on runs high above the beach so I feel as if I can see for miles. I look down at the crystal blue water and can't wait to enjoy it. I watch as gentle white waves slowly wash over the sand. The ocean is calm today. It is perfect for swimming.

David slows the car and switches on the turn signal. He pulls into a sandy little parking lot between two houses. The warm ocean breeze gently blows sand back and forth across the pavement.

"I'd better put the top up quickly before the whole car is full of sand," David says and pushes the button. I wait until it is closed to open the door and then step out of the car. Tiny grains of sand tickle my ankles and feet as I walk around to the back of the car. I slip my flip-flops off my feet and slide them down into my beach bag. David kicks off his own shoes and wiggles his toes down into a pile of soft sand.

Barefoot is the only way to walk onto a beach.

chapter 3
Sandy Toes

DAVID LIFTS our chairs out of the car and underneath I notice for the first time that he's also packed a colorful beach umbrella. He picks this up as well and starts stumbling toward the beach.

"Here, let me carry something," I say and hold out my empty hand. He gratefully passes one of the chairs to me and we continue our search for an empty spot where we can place our things.

The beach is pretty crowded because it is a Saturday. Everywhere there are pockets of people enjoying the beautiful sunny day.

I let my eyes roam over the scene and I see a perfect little spot for two people. I tell David to follow me and I lead us almost to the water's edge.

A seagull dips down from the sky and lands on the sand near my feet. He bends his head to snap up someone's discarded potato chip. The bird squawks and waddles closer to me.

"Shoo!" I say. "We don't have any potato chips to share. You're out of luck." I wave my hand at the bird to scare him away but he just stands and stares at me. I shrug and turn my attention to setting up my chair.

I sit down to test it out and giggle as the cool foamy water bubbles over my bare toes. The water is colder than I expected but it is a nice contrast to the hot sun. David sits down beside me with a sigh and for a moment we are just quiet.

"Let's enjoy the sun a bit before we set up the umbrella, ok?" I ask. David nods. I wiggle my feet side to side until they are completely buried under the sand. With each coming wave, the pile of sand is washed away. I enjoy the sensation.

In the distance, just beyond the reach of the waves, a large blue fishing boat bobs on the ocean. I watch as a tall man stands on the front of the boat, gathering something in his arms.

In one quick motion, he casts a giant fishing net out into the ocean. It sinks out of sight for a moment. The tall man in the front of the boat is joined by another man, and the two of them start to haul the net back out of the water.

Even though the men are far away I can see the muscles in their arms standing out as they lift the heavy net from the sea. It is now full of wiggling silver-scaled fish. As the fish flop against each other in the net, their scales blink in the bright sunlight and remind me of a disco ball.

Finally, the men get the net all the way in the boat and I can no longer see the fish. There is a distant hum as the boat's motor starts back up and one man steers it further away from shore.

By this time the sun is beginning to sink into my skin. I feel the familiar burn of its rays. I reach into my bag and take out a little bottle of sunscreen. As I spray it on my arms and legs, its coconut smell reminds me of childhood vacations long past and fun times with my friends when we were younger.

"Isn't this nice?" I ask David. He mumbles a response, seeming to be half asleep already.

"Here, you better put some of this on if you're going to nap out here," I say and pass the bottle of sunscreen over to him.

"Thanks," he says, taking the bottle. I shield my eyes and make sure to keep my mouth closed as he sprays his arms. It may smell delicious, but it definitely doesn't taste good!

A gust of wind brings a bright red bucket tumbling up to my feet. I quickly reach down to grab it and look around for its owner. A little boy, runs up to me. He is out of breath and a lady who must be his mother is trailing along behind him.

"Is this yours?" I ask him, holding out the bucket.

He nods his little blond head and takes the bucket from me.

"I'm building the biggest sandcastle on the whole beach," he says and makes a grand movement with his arms.

"Well, I would love to see it when you're done."

"Ok, me and my mom are right back here," he says, pointing to a spot not far behind us.

"Great, you come let me know when you're finished and I'll come see it."

chapter 4
Swim Time

THE BOY skips off, swinging his bucket and kicking up little sprays of sand behind his feet. By this time, I am quite hot and ready to take a swim.

I stand up from my chair and with only a few steps I am knee-deep in the salty water. I try to keep my balance as wave after wave sucks the sand from under my feet. David laughs as I wobble and throw my arms out to the side for balance.

I walk on into the ocean and am now waist deep. I pick up my feet and let the water hold me.

There are people in the water next to me and I hear small pieces of conversation as I bob up and down.

A family with a baby float beside me. The baby sits in a little boat shaped like a frog. She pats the frog's green head and happily splashes her tiny feet in the water. I love her laugh. I smile at her mother and father and swim deeper into the sea.

When the water reaches my chest, I stop. This time, I pick my feet all the way up to the water's surface and let myself float on my back. I feel like a kid again.

I let my arms fall out to the side of my body and just give myself to the ocean. It is so peaceful. My ears are under the water so all is quiet. Gently, my body dips up and down on the calm ocean.

A piece of slimy green seaweed has wrapped around my arm. I watch it wave in the water for a second before pulling it off.

After a moment, I stand back up and wave to David so he will join me. He waves back and I see him stand from his chair. He holds up one finger to tell me to wait and he walks to a stand at the back of the beach. In this area, there are toys, chairs, food, drinks, and other things for sale.

I cannot see what David is doing but it becomes clear when he walks into the water to meet me. He has a bright green float tucked under each arm. Each one is long enough to lie on and I am happy he has brought them into the water.

My legs are getting tired and I am thankful for a float to sit on in the water.

"It will be easier to get on this in the shallow water," David says. We walk toward the beach and I find he is right. I swing my leg over the float and plop down.

Somehow, I manage to not fall off. I use my legs to push myself back out into the deeper water. Once I can no longer touch the bottom, I lie back and get comfortable on the float.

David suggests we hold hands so we don't float apart. I agree that this is a good idea.

As I lie on the float and look up at the sky I see two large birds fly over our heads. I think I remember what they're called. Pelicans. The birds have very large pouches below their beaks. As I watch, one of them swoops down into the water to catch a fish.

The water that drips from the bird's beak glitters in the sun and looks beautiful. I hope he caught himself a nice lunch, I think. Thinking of the bird eating makes my stomach growl.

"Are you getting hungry?" I ask David.

"Yes, a little," he says. "I packed some crackers and fruit in my bag. When we get ready to get out we can have a little snack. Sound good?"

"Yep. That's works for me," I reply.

I'm not quite hungry enough to go back to the beach just yet. I am perfectly relaxed bobbing in the gentle waves.

As I look towards the beach, I notice the little blond boy building his sandcastle. He is happily sitting, covered in sand, in the middle of dozens of small mounds. Even from the water, I can see bright flags fluttering on top of them. His mother is sitting nearby reading a book.

I enjoy watching them for a minute and remember making my own sandcastles.

I also think back on long ago vacations where my friends and I would get sunburns from staying in the water so long. We would talk about everything you could imagine and would never want to come in.

Being at the beach always makes me wish I lived at the beach. As we float, I daydream about just that. I picture a cute little beach cottage with a front porch swing facing the water. I would love to spend my evenings sitting on that porch, watching the sunset over the sea.

chapter 5
Let's Eat

SOON I BEGIN to notice a new smell in the salty air. I raise my head and scan the beach to see where it is coming from. It doesn't take long to find the source of the delicious smell.

A brightly colored truck sits parked at the back of the beach. A picture of a cartoon taco decorates the side of the truck. There is also a window that slides open. I can see people moving around and cooking inside.

Yellow, green, and blue flags wave in the wind on top of the truck. I see a line beginning to form in front of the open window.

"Ok, I'm definitely hungry now," I say. "I think we should swim back to the beach and get some tacos."

"Tacos?" David mumbles and I can see he was almost asleep on his float. He lifts his head now too and looks at where I'm pointing. I can see by the look on his face that the delicious smell has reached him also.

The smell is full of rich spices and the warm scent of meat cooking on a buttered grill. I think I can smell peppers and onions as well. I can see steam rising from a vent in the top of the truck.

David breathes in deeply and makes a silly face. He licks his lips and rubs his hand over his stomach and nods.

"My belly is telling me that tacos sound like a great idea," he says, "forget the boring crackers and fruit. Let's get some real food!"

We both swing our legs over the sides of our floats and begin half-walking, half-swimming back to the shore. We let the strong waves push against our backs and use that force to speed up our trip back to the sand.

My own stomach begins to rumble as we get closer. Walking gets harder as the water gets more shallow so David and I lean on one another to keep from falling down. I am sure we look pretty funny as we stumble over the uneven sand.

I lift my legs high to try to step over the waves and not get pulled back into the deeper water. In this clumsy way, we finally make it out of the water.

We dry off a little and stack our floats beside our chairs. I roll my towel back up and put it back in my bag so it doesn't get covered in sand. David opens his bag and takes out his wallet.

"I'm starving all of a sudden," he says as we make our way to the end of the line at the taco truck.

There are only four people in line ahead of us, so our wait is not very long. I read the menu as we stand and decide I will order a chicken and cheese taco with sour cream, refried beans and avocado on top. My mouth waters just thinking about it.

When it is our turn, I let David place our order. The lady at the window asks if we want anything to drink. An ice-cold Coca-Cola sounds perfect to me, so I tell her so.

On the right side of the truck, there are four picnic tables. One is empty, so we get our food and go sit. We can watch our belongings from here and have a more comfortable place to eat.

Next to us, a family of five laughs and talks loudly. They seem to be having such a good time I can't help but smile at them.

A little boy smiles back at me and waves his chubby hand. I wave at him and continue eating my taco.

It is not long before all our food is gone and our bellies are full. We clean up our trash and throw it in the garbage can.

It has been such a nice afternoon so far. David and I walk back to our chairs and settle in to soak up some more sun. The food and sun together have made me sleepy.

I let my mind rest as I watch two kites fly in the breeze. One is shaped like a dragon. Its tail is made of rainbow-colored streamers that trail behind it in the strong wind.

I trace the line down from the sky to a girl who looks about fourteen years old. She holds tightly to the kite handle and runs along the beach, splashing in the edge of the water and kicking up sand behind her bare feet. My eyes begin to close as she gets further away and for a while, I just doze.

chapter 6
Sunset

BEING AT the beach today has brought back so many wonderful memories. Happy family memories of vacations as a child, good times with friends, and the pleasure of making new memories now.

It doesn't seem possible that our afternoon is coming to an end, but as I sit in my chair and watch the ocean I see the sun sinking closer and closer to the water.

The setting sun has turned the clouds a million beautiful colors. Pink and purple fluff floating gently across a darkening sky. I slide my sunglasses up on my head so that I can take in this amazing sight more clearly.

The sun is close enough to the water now that it appears to be melting into the sea. It spreads its orange fire along the far edge of the water.

"Look," David whispers to me.

I look out into the ocean and can see a pod of dolphins playing. I see their smooth bodies leap out of the water, one after another. It looks as if there are about five of them. They swim so fast they quickly move out of sight, but it is such a joy to see them splashing around.

"Oh, how amazing," I say. "I haven't seen dolphins here since I was a kid."

David smiles at me. "Have you enjoyed yourself today?" he asks.

"Very much," I answer.

"Me too. I think it is about time to pack up and head home though, don't you?"

"Yes. I suppose we should. It will be dark soon."

I stand up and begin to gather my belongings. David does the same. We take extra care to not leave anything behind.

I take one last long look at the sky and the water and the beach. I breathe in deeply one more time and feel so content with myself.

On our way out, we pass a group of young people gathered around a small bonfire. They laugh and talk in loud voices. I see the girls toss their long hair in the firelight and see the boys doing stunts and flips on the sand to impress those girls. I think back to being that young.

There is a shower head attached to a post near the parking area. David and I stop to rinse our feet and legs before we get in his car. The water is colder than the ocean and gives me goosebumps. I pat my feet dry with my pink towel and slide my flip-flops back on my feet.

Once we have loaded the trunk we climb in and begin the drive back home. I watch out the window as the sky continues to fade from blue to gray to black.

"Thanks for taking me to the beach today," I say to David. He nods and pats my knee.

"It was a lot of fun," he says.

We pull into the driveway and unload our things. David hangs the chairs back on their hooks and I throw our towels and bathing suits in the washing machine. Once those chores are completed, I walk upstairs to take a nice warm shower.

There is no other feeling that compares to the feel of your skin after a nice day at the beach. The sand has smoothed the rough parts and the sun has given me a little glow. I study myself in the mirror before stepping into the shower and am filled with happiness again.

The shower is so warm on my sunbaked skin that I just stand there under the spray and let the sand and sweat slide off my body.

I look forward to sliding between my crisp, clean sheets tonight. The sun has a way of zapping your energy and making you tired in a very special way.

My day at the beach has been very special. Time spent with those you love is always a good thing. I know I will fall into a deep, contented sleep tonight replaying the day in my head.

THE END

A Day At the Beach – Chapter Summaries

Chapter 1 - A Lovely Idea

David and I are sitting together on the sun porch, eating, when David suggests we go to the beach. We are planning a trip to the beach, and I am excited to see the ocean and feel the sand between my toes...

Chapter 2 - Taking a Ride

David's convertible is a beautiful car with smooth gray leather seats and I feel as happy as a child on vacation. We drive to the beach. The ocean is calm and the sand is soft, making it perfect for swimming...

Chapter 3 - Sandy Toes

We walk to the beach and find a perfect spot for two people. A seagull approaches us. David sits down beside me and we enjoy the sun before setting up the umbrella. The sun is lovely on my skin, and a boy is building a big sandcastle on the beach...

Chapter 4 - Swim Time

I take a swim in the ocean and see a family with a baby. I relax in the waves, watching a little blond boy build a sandcastle, and daydream about a beach cottage with a front porch swing...

Chapter 5 - Let's Eat

David and I walk to a taco truck and order a chicken and cheese taco with sour cream, refried beans and avocado on top. We watch two kites fly in the breeze and enjoy the sun...

Chapter 6 - Sunset

We enjoy our afternoon at the beach, where we see a pod of dolphins playing and a group of young people gathered around a bonfire. I take a warm shower after a day at the beach, feeling refreshed and content. Time spent with those you love is always a good thing...

THE END

SHORT STORIES

Delightful short stories
all about beaches.

Short Story - Walking My Dog

THE SUN GLINTED off the water as I walked along the beach with my beloved dog, Max. The sand felt cool beneath my feet and the breeze was gentle on my skin. I felt a sense of peace and tranquility wash over me as I watched the waves lap against the shoreline.

Max trotted ahead of me, sniffing at the occasional seaweed or odd shell here and there. Every now and then, he'd glance back at me and wag his tail, as if to say, "Isn't this great?"

We continued along, stopping every now and then to explore an interesting rock formation or inspect a particularly intriguing piece of driftwood.

As we walked, I couldn't help but be taken aback by the stunning beauty of the landscape around us. The ocean was a deep blue, stretching out as far as the eye could see. The shoreline was littered with shells and rocks of all shapes and sizes, each one a unique and fascinating treasure.

The salty sea air tickled my nose and I breathed in deeply, savoring the feeling of contentment that settled over me. Max seemed to feel it too, as he pranced along with an extra spring in his step. We continued on, taking our time, not wanting the moment to end.

As we rounded a bend, I noticed a small rocky outcropping off in the distance. We decided to investigate and quickly found ourselves on the edge of an inlet.

The water was so still and calm that it seemed almost inviting. I stepped in cautiously, letting the cool water lap gently around my ankles. Max was right beside me, his eyes alive with excitement.

We explored the inlet, marveling at the abundance of sea life around us. Schools of fish swam around us and the occasional crab crawled in and out of little crevices.

Max even spotted a couple of sea stars, their intricate patterns glistening in the sunlight. I felt a sense of pure wonder and amazement, something I hadn't felt in a long time.

We eventually reached the other side of the inlet and made our way back to shore. We continued along the beach, pausing occasionally to admire the beauty of the ocean. As we walked, I felt a deep sense of appreciation for the world around me. Eventually, our walk came to an end and we turned back, making our way slowly back to the car.

As we drove home, I felt a sense of satisfaction. Despite not having gone very far, I felt as if I had explored a whole new world and made some wonderful discoveries along the way.

I looked out the window and watched as the sun slowly set over the horizon, content and at peace with the world.

Max slept peacefully in the back seat, his head resting gently against my shoulder. I found myself smiling, grateful for this beautiful moment, grateful for my dog, Max.

THE END

Short Story - Beach Vacation

OUR DAY BEGAN before the sun had even risen. It was still cool out, and the sky was still dark, but there was a hint of pink on the horizon.

We had decided to make the most of our vacation with an early start to the beach. I had packed a delicious picnic lunch, complete with sandwiches, drinks, snacks and a blanket to sit on.

We arrived at the beach just as the sun was beginning to peak over the horizon. The sand was still cool and damp, and I could feel the mist in the air as the waves lapped against the shoreline. We spread out the blanket and settled down to enjoy the moment. The view was spectacular and the sound of the waves was a calming melody.

As the sun rose higher in the sky, the temperature began to climb, and soon it was warm enough to take off our jackets and shoes. We rolled up our pants and t-shirts and spread out our lunch. The sandwiches were a delicious combination of fresh vegetables, crunchy pickles and mayo, and the drinks were refreshing and cool.

The waves had grown in size since we had arrived, and the surfers were out in full force. We watched in awe as they gracefully glided along the crests and dips of the water, their grace and skill undeniable.

We spent the morning chatting, snacking, and soaking up the sun. The day had taken on a slow and leisurely pace, and it was incredibly relaxing. It seemed that all the worries of the world had melted away, and all that remained was the present.

At lunch time, we ate the sandwiches we had brought, and chatted some more. The sun was hot, but the breeze was cool, and the sensation was a perfect balance. We talked about everything, from life in general to the funny stories that we had heard.

Eventually, we decided to take a walk along the beach. We picked up some shells, and noted the different sea birds that were flying over the water. The smells of the ocean air filled our noses, and it was like a breath of fresh air.

As the sun began to set, we decided it was time to leave. We packed up our picnic, and made our way back to the car. We both agreed that it had been a wonderful day.

The next day, we decided to head back to the beach. We had such a wonderful time yesterday that we wanted to do it all over again. We drove down to the beach in anticipation, the windows down, the breeze blowing through our hair.

When we arrived, the beach was already crowded. People were everywhere, and the sun was shining brightly. We spread out our blanket and set up our picnic once again.

This time, we had brought some board games to play, and some beach umbrellas to offer shade. We set up our game and played for a few hours, the laughter and chatter of our friends keeping us entertained.

The afternoon was spent lazily, lounging on the sand, reading books, and listening to music. We moved our blanket around, checking out different areas of the beach and taking in the scenery. We even stopped to watch a volleyball game that was happening nearby.

The sun was beginning to dip in the sky as we packed up our things for the day. We said goodbye to the beach and began making our way back to the car. We drove home feeling content and relaxed, the events of the day playing back in our minds.

The third day of our trip to the beach was much different from the first two. We arrived later in the morning, and the beach was already lined with beachgoers. We spread out our blanket in a less populated area and began to enjoy our day.

The sun was shining brightly, and the waves were crashing against the shoreline. We watched as people splashed around in the ocean, and listened to the laughter of children playing in the sand.

We spent the afternoon playing cards, and swimming in the ocean. The waves were cool and refreshing, and we felt relaxed and content. The sun was beginning to set, and the sky was painted with a beautiful array of colors.

We decided to take a walk along the beach as the sun began to dip beneath the horizon. We stopped to look at shells, and jump over the waves. I could feel the sand between my toes and the warmth of the sun on my skin. We soaked up the last moments of the day, and breathed in the salty air.

As we returned to the blanket, I realized just how much I had enjoyed the day. We had spent the day with our friends, and been able to relax and appreciate the beauty of the beach.

The fourth and final day of our trip to the beach was bittersweet. We knew that our time here was coming to an end, and that soon it would be time to go.

We arrived at the beach a little later in the morning, and the sun was already high in the sky. We spread out our blanket and settled down, the warmth of the sand beneath us.

We spent the day sunbathing, and enjoying the sound of the waves. We chatted and laughed, and played some more cards. We watched as people swam and surfed, and kids built sandcastles.

At lunchtime, we ate the picnic lunch we had brought with us. The sandwiches were delicious, and the drinks were cold and refreshing. We talked about our time here, and the memories we had made.

As the sun began to set, we knew it was time to go. We packed our things, and said goodbye to the beach. We had had such a wonderful time, and the memories would stay with us forever.

We climbed into the car and drove away, the sound of the waves fading in the background. We were both sad to be leaving, but we had fond memories and a newfound appreciation of the beauty of the beach.

THE END

Short Story - Beach Book

I'M SITTING on the beach, the sun glaring down on my pale skin, the ocean waves crashing in the distance. The sound of the sea is a calming one, and I feel my eyes drooping as I relax into my chair. I had decided to spend my day here at the beach, and I had made a perfect plan. I had brought a book with me, a novel I had been meaning to read, and the perfect spot to put my blanket and sit down.

I opened up my book, and as I began to read, I felt my stress slowly ebb away. The words were a balm for my soul, and I felt my mind wander to a place of calm and tranquility. I felt the tension in my shoulders ease and my breathing become even as I completely immersed myself in the world of the novel.

I settled comfortably into my chair, taking in the view of the shoreline before me. The sound of the waves lapped at the shore and the seagulls cawed in the sky. For the first time in what felt like forever, I felt completely relaxed. I continued to read, and I felt myself drift into a world of fantasy and imagination. It was a world that opened up so many possibilities, and I felt my spirit soar as I read.

The sun was slowly shifting in the sky, and I glanced up to watch its rays glint off the ocean. I could feel the warmth of the sun beating down on my face, and I closed my eyes to take in the beauty of the moment. I felt my entire body relax as I let go of all my worries and stress. I was totally present in this moment, and I felt so alive and content.

The smell of the ocean wafted over me as I continued to read, and I felt my whole body become completely at ease. I was completely in tune with nature, and I felt a sense of peace wash over me. I felt the sand beneath my toes, and I could smell the sea salt in the air. I was totally immersed in the beauty of the moment, and nothing else mattered.

The hours slowly ticked by as I continued to read, and I felt my body sink further into the chair. I felt a sense of peace come over me that I hadn't felt in a long time. I was so consumed in my book that I wasn't even aware of the time, and eventually I felt my eyes getting heavy. I slowly closed my book and let out a deep sigh of contentment.

I had spent the day surrounded by nature and the soothing sound of the ocean, and I felt like I had just had the most relaxing day ever. All my worries had faded away and I felt like I could face anything that came my way. I had found a sense of peace and tranquility, and I was so grateful for the experience.

I stood up and stretched my limbs, feeling the sand cushion my feet as I walked closer to the shore. I looked out at the horizon, my eyes following the line of the sea as far as they could reach. I took in a deep breath of the salty air and felt a wave of calm come over me.

I smiled as I turned away from the sea and made my way back to my blanket. I folded it up and tucked my book inside. I knew that I would be back soon, to sit on the beach and escape into the pages of a book.

I walked away, feeling a sense of contentment and peace. I had found a new sense of balance and calm, and I was so grateful. I had spent my day totally focused on the present moment, and I was amazed at how much better I felt from it. I was now ready to take on whatever life threw at me, and for that I was truly thankful.

THE END

Short Story - Beach Laughter

I SIT CROSS-LEGGED on the sand, my toes in a pile of sand, my fingers intertwined in my lap. The sun is warm on my skin, yet the salty breeze is cool and refreshing against my face. I can hear the laughter of children playing tag on the beach, their chubby legs and arms running back and forth in the sand. Despite the perfect summer day, I feel the weight of the years behind me, the memories of the past and present.

For a moment, I am transported back to my childhood, the warm days spent at the beach watching children play, with kites flying and sandcastles built. I can feel the familiar nostalgia of youthful innocence, of a carefree life with never ending possibilities.

My gaze follows the children playing tag, their laughter ringing out like bells in the air. They are racing back and forth, their faces alight with joy and laughter, their plaintive cries of "not it!" ringing out. It is a scene of pure joy and innocence, a scene that transports me away from my troubles, my worries, and my responsibilities.

I watch as one of the children catches the beach ball and turns to throw it to another. The ball is bright and colorful, bouncing off the sand and into the hands of another child. I am filled with a sense of peace and contentment, watching the children play and laugh.

Off in the distance I can see an old man sitting in the sand, a fishing rod in hand.

I can almost feel him, his attention focused intently on the horizon, waiting for the tell-tale tug of a caught fish. It is a peaceful scene, and I am filled with a quiet admiration for the man, and his ability to find peace and relaxation in this simple activity.

The sun is beating down on my face now, and I am conscious of the sound of the waves crashing onto the shore. It is a soothing rhythm, and I feel myself slowly relaxing into it, the stress of the day slowly draining away.

My gaze drifts back to the children, who are now playing a game of catch. The sand is flying up from their feet as they race around, arms outstretched to catch the beach ball as it sails in the air. The sound of their laughter is infectious, and I find myself joining in, my heart light and my spirit free.

I am filled with a sense of joy and contentment, and I find myself wondering at the beauty of life and its simple pleasures. The children are my reminder of life's possibilities.

The sun is beginning to set and the children have run off, their laughter a distant memory. I sit and watch the waves, my soul at peace, my heart full. I take a deep breath and fill my lungs with the salty air, and as I do so, I feel myself relax and sink into the sand, the memories of the day washing over me in a wave of peaceful contentment.

I am filled with a deep joy, and I find myself wishing that this moment could last forever. I know that it can't, but it doesn't stop me from wanting it to.

I sit and watch the sun setting, a beautiful array of colors spilling across the sky in a magnificent display of beauty. I know that this moment is fleeting, and I treasure it, knowing that it will soon be gone.

The sun is gone now, and I reluctantly rise from the sand. I take one last look at the beach, the sand and the sea, the memories of the day lingering in my mind. I will carry them with me, and I know that these memories will bring me comfort and joy for years to come.

As I walk away, I leave with a smile on my face, and a feeling of peace in my heart. I know that I will cherish this day forever, and that I will always have my memories of sand, sunshine, and laughter.

THE END

Short Story - Message in a Bottle

I LED THE WAY, the child following me, his small hands in mine. The sand was cool, rippling beneath our feet, and a breeze softly blew against our faces. We moved towards the horizon, where the sun was setting in the distant sky.

The beach was alive with sounds and movement. Crashing waves rolled in, the endless sea beating against the shore. Tiny crabs scuttled along the sand, and sandpipers ran in circles, probing for food. Further out, seagulls flew overhead, their cries echoing in the air.

As we continued along, I paused to examine the various treasures washed up in the tide. Here was an old boot, its leather cracked and worn. There was a rusty anchor, its chain tied to an empty bottle. Further away, I spotted a piece of driftwood, its smooth surface slowly eroding away.

The child seemed fascinated by what lay scattered across the shore. He pointed out tiny shells, and stopped to pick up a stranded jellyfish. He squatted down to inspect a tiny crab, and followed after a wave as it retreated back into the sea.

The sky began to darken as the sun sank lower, casting a golden light on the sand. I felt the child's hand tighten around mine, as if he was trying to hold onto the moment. We continued walking, and then suddenly I felt something tug at my arm.

The child had stopped, his eyes wide with wonder. He was pointing to something barely visible in the sand. I followed his gaze and saw a small glass bottle, its bright green color glinting in the fading light. I bent down to pick it up and the child ran towards it, eager to see what was inside.

The bottle had a cork stopper in the top, and inside was a tiny rolled-up piece of paper. I carefully unrolled it, smoothing out the wrinkles. Written on it in barely legible handwriting were the words:

"A thousand chances."

I looked at the child and smiled. "It's a message," I said. "It means that no matter what happens, you always have a chance to try again, to make something new of your life."

He looked up at me, his eyes shining. "Really?" he asked.

I nodded. "Really. We all have a thousand chances."

We continued our walk, the child's little hand in mine, the bottle in the other. I looked down at him, my heart full with love and joy. A thousand chances, I thought. Yes, a thousand chances.

THE END

WORD SEARCH

Exercise your brain with a word search.
Good luck!

Need a paper copy? Download and print the
word search puzzles and coloring pages
contained in this book by visiting:
seniorality.com/a-day-at-the-beach

PUZZLE 1 – BEACH WORD SEARCH

```
Y U W P E A C E F U L R R Y G W L
S O V K W Q H N P K P E A P K B Z
K I L U D Q H J U O F O X V U D J
T T U P U M Q A V O B V V J X J R
K R N L N V A C A T I O N W O W C
X Z C P E W X T O H H C H S C B O
A L H O S J N Z P C G P F U K M A
Z B J U H X P W O M O J J V D L S
Z J S V Z L L A A U D E S Q L K T
D H B F W O N D E R F U L X G X L
O N S W S T R X U M B R E L L A I
C T Y Z P O T W W E T E H H C V N
E Z T O V W B A A E T B E A C H E
A M G X V E I W T H F I S H I N G
N F M Z O L R E E C S F L O A T V
E H M P R A H A R A X A N F T G G
O I F R J C R P I C N I C Y U G K
```

BEACH   PEACEFUL
COASTLINE   PICNIC
DUNES   TOWEL
FISHING   UMBRELLA
FLOAT   VACATION
LUNCH   WATER
OCEAN   WONDERFUL

PUZZLE 2 – SUPER S WORD SEARCH

```
Z  A  W  K  F  S  U  R  F  T  C  O  J  S  S  K  S
H  S  Z  D  O  V  E  B  M  S  W  I  M  B  H  Y  S
E  A  D  O  N  N  O  R  Q  K  J  C  D  I  I  Z  B
V  U  Z  T  Q  F  U  Y  R  C  G  K  B  D  R  K  K
S  N  L  L  C  S  U  N  S  C  R  E  E  N  T  N  P
B  C  X  C  A  P  S  A  N  D  W  I  C  H  H  U  N
S  C  W  E  S  U  N  S  E  T  K  I  Y  J  H  Q  Y
Z  X  Q  S  H  O  R  E  O  U  S  H  O  R  T  S  Z
Q  T  Y  M  Y  W  B  S  U  N  G  L  A  S  S  E  S
K  W  W  P  Y  U  J  S  I  D  B  U  G  L  J  I  Z
L  M  E  G  S  R  K  U  O  D  N  U  O  Y  X  S  Q
S  S  A  N  D  F  Q  N  R  F  M  S  B  P  T  M  K
O  S  A  N  D  C  A  S  T  L  E  R  E  T  M  D  G
L  B  F  Q  W  A  J  H  V  S  H  A  D  E  W  M  I
A  Y  M  K  G  B  D  I  M  U  S  M  I  L  E  S  N
E  K  E  Q  S  Q  G  N  L  P  P  U  E  F  F  K  L
X  E  N  J  I  K  S  E  R  Z  W  N  S  O  U  B  M
```

SAND	SMILES
SANDCASTLE	SUNGLASSES
SANDWICH	SUNSCREEN
SHADE	SUNSET
SHIRT	SUNSHINE
SHORE	SURF
SHORTS	SWIM

SOLUTION 1 – BEACH

SOLUTION 2 – SUPER S

COLORING PAGES

Relax with these calming coloring pages, inpired by this book. Enjoy!

Need a paper copy? Download and print the word search puzzles and coloring pages contained in this book by visiting:

seniorality.com/a-day-at-the-beach

COLOR THE BEACH SCENE

COLOR THE ICE CREAM

THANK YOU

Visit **seniorality.com** for access to a wide range of books, stories, word searches, coloring pages, audio book videos, a monthly magazine, and more.

LAUNCHING IN SEPTEMBER 2023

ORDER YOUR MAGAZINE NOW
seniorality.com

Printed in Great Britain
by Amazon

34474057R00058